In the Garden

BY ELIZABETH LANG

The Child's World

Published by The Child's World®
1980 Lookout Drive • Mankato, MN 56003-1705
800-599-READ • www.childsworld.com

Acknowledgments
The Child's World®: Mary Berendes, Publishing Director
Red Line Editorial: Editorial direction
The Design Lab: Design
Amnet: Production
Photographs ©:Front cover: BrandX, Comstock; BrandX, 2, 3, 4, 6,
12, 13, 15, 16, 23; Shutterstock/Gorillaimages, 5; Comstock, 7, 21;
FoodIcons, 8, 19; Shutterstock/Zocchi Roberto, 9; DigitalStock, 10, 18,
21; iStockPhoto, 12; PhotoDisc, 14; Shutterstock/Catalin Petolea, 17;
Shutterstock/Olga Pedan, 21

ISBN: 978-1623235420
LCCN: 2013931338

Printed in the United States of America
Mankato, MN
July, 2013
PA02174

ABOUT THE AUTHOR

Elizabeth Lang is a writer, artist, and teacher. She lives in Olympia, Washington, with her husband, three children, three cats, two dogs, and a great deal of rain.

Table of Contents

CHAPTER ONE

Gifts of a Garden

It's not fair. You have been playing outside for hours, and your stomach is growling from hunger. You look over your fence and see your neighbor stuffing her mouth with juicy, red strawberries. Now she's plucking fat, crispy snow peas from the vine. Oh, no, there she goes biting into a plump, crunchy carrot. You've had it. It's time to grow your *own* garden!

A garden is a plot of ground where herbs, fruits, flowers, or vegetables grow. It can be as small as your windowsill or as large as a football field.

▶ **Opposite page: You can grow a garden in your yard, on your patio, or even on a windowsill.**

▼ **Strawberries are one of many foods you can grow in your own garden.**

You can grow a garden in your yard, inside a tractor tire, on a rooftop or balcony, and even on a fire escape.

There are different kinds of gardens. Water gardens, shade gardens, herb gardens, and rock gardens are some of the many gardens you can grow. But most gardens do have something in common: They are good for us.

Garden plants help the environment the way all plants do—they absorb **carbon dioxide** and release **oxygen**. Fruits and vegetables are packed with **vitamins**, **fiber**, and other **nutrients** that help protect you from disease. People who garden say it is relaxing. They enjoy the

▼ *Carrots provide many essential nutrients.*

fresh air and exercise. People who grow vegetable gardens eat more vegetables. Are you ready to eat your own plump and crunchy carrots? Let's grow!

CHAPTER TWO

Planning Your Garden

Is there a sunny patch of ground in your yard or patio? All vegetables need sunlight. Your garden will need at least six to eight hours of sunlight each day. Also, choose a spot that is close to a water source. If a hose can reach your garden, watering will be easier. Lastly, every garden starts with the soil. That does not mean you just throw a bunch of seeds into the dirt and watch them grow. You need healthy soil with lots of nutrients to help your food grow.

▲ All these vegetables start with healthy soil.

▶ Opposite page: Soil with lots of nutrients will produce beautiful vegetables like these.

Healthy Soil

There are three basic types of soil **particles**: sand, silt, and clay. The size of a particle will help you understand how well your soil will drain. It can also tell you how well the soil will hold nutrients. Sand is the largest type of soil particle. It feels rough when you rub it. Sand does not hold many nutrients. Silt is a soil particle that is smaller than sand but bigger than clay. When you rub silt, it feels smooth and chalky. Clay is the smallest soil particle. It is gummy when wet and smooth when dry. Clay can hold nutrients, but it is hard for air and water to get through it.

Here is a test to see if the soil is right for your garden. After a week of dry weather, find a long-handled garden spade. Push the spade straight down into the soil in a few spots where you plan

▼ *Use a rake like this one to break up thick soil.*

WONDERFUL WORMS

Worms are great garden helpers. They are covered with thousands of tiny hairs that help them move in the soil. Worms increase the amount of air and water in the soil, and their waste is filled with nutrients. These little wigglers help build healthier soil.

to put your garden. If you have to jump up and down on the spade, the soil is too thick. If it sinks in easily, the soil may be too sandy and light. If you have to press your foot on the spade but the soil lifts, you probably have good soil.

You can also test the soil by getting your hands dirty. Soil that is hard and does not break apart easily in your hand is probably clay. If soil feels gritty in your hand and does not stay in a clump, it is probably too sandy. However, if the soil clumps but will also break apart, you probably have good soil.

Soil is a living, breathing material. Your soil needs air, water, and nutrients. You may have found a spot in your yard with good soil for your garden, but you will need to feed it to keep it that way. Do you have eggshells or banana peels? You can use them and some leaves to make compost. Compost is the **humus** left over from plants after they have **decomposed**. Putting a scoop of compost on your soil is like giving it vitamins.

New gardeners can make compost in five easy steps:

1. Find a spot outside to make your compost pile. Add leaves, grass cuttings, and yard trimmings.

2. Find a large container or pail with a lid (a coffee tin works well). Place it on the kitchen counter where you can reach it.

3. Fill your pail with vegetable and fruit peels, eggshells, tea bags, and coffee grounds. Do not put meat, bones, eggs, or dairy foods in your pail. These scraps bring rats and other pests.

▲ *Banana peels and eggshells are good ingredients for compost.*

4. When your pail is full, dump it onto your pile.

5. Add more leaves, grass cuttings, and yard trimmings. Now and then, you will need to stir the pile with a garden fork.

Choosing Your Veggies

Many vegetables are easy to grow. But, vegetables do not just appear in your garden, ready to eat. You have to start with seeds. Try to buy high-quality seeds. Many seed companies sell **organic** seeds. Most importantly, choose vegetables you will want to eat!

Here is a list of easy-to-grow vegetables:

- Baby carrots
- Green beans

▲ *Potatoes, beans, and radishes are just a few of the vegetables you can grow in a garden.*

13

- Lettuce
- Potatoes
- Radishes
- Spinach

When choosing the seeds for your vegetables, think about where you live. Some vegetables like warm **climates**, while others like cool climates. If you live in a southern state such as Florida,

◄ *Tomatoes grow well in warm weather.*

OUTSTANDING ONIONS

Onions have played an important role in cultures all over the world. Onions were used to treat gunshot wounds for hundreds of years. During the American Civil War, General Ulysses S. Grant would not move his troops without a supply of onions. An old English rhyme says that the thickness of an onion skin can predict the winter. A thin skin means a mild winter, and a thick skin means watch out: rough winter ahead!

▶ *Onions are popular all over the world.*

you want seeds that grow well in sandy soil and extreme heat. If you live in a northern state such as Colorado, you need seeds that will grow in cold weather and in hard soil with a lot of clay. If you live in a place as cold as Antarctica, you'll have to start a **greenhouse**. The ground is too cold!

CHAPTER THREE

Ready? Set? Plant!

▼ *You may need boots like these to stay dry while planting your seeds.*

Once you have found your garden spot, made your compost, chosen your vegetables, and bought your seeds, it is time to start planting. A vegetable garden usually cannot be planted in one day. Some seeds should be planted in cool weather and others when it is warmer. You can find planting schedules online or in gardening books and magazines.

When to plant also depends on where you live. In northern climates, it is often best to plant in the spring. Planting in September works well in many climates, too. Roots grow well in soil that has

▲ *Grow garlic from cloves planted three inches (7.5 cm) deep and six inches (15 cm) apart.*

warmed up over the summer. In warmer climates you can often plant year-round.

Making Your Rows

Different vegetables need different planting plans. For example, you plant three carrot seeds for every inch of your row, but you plant only one or two spinach seeds per inch. Use your fingers and feet to space your seeds, plant them at the right depth, and space the rows apart. All you need is a ruler.

To find the planting depth:

1. Measure the tip of your index finger to the first joint. How long is it (in inches)?
2. Measure the tip of your finger to the second joint. How long is it?
3. Measure your whole finger. How long is it?

To find the distance you need to plant between seeds:

1. Measure the width of your index and middle finger when they are together. How wide are they (in inches)?
2. Measure the width of your three middle fingers when they are together. How wide are they?
3. How about four fingers? How wide are they?
4. How far can you stretch your thumb and index finger?

Lastly, use the length of two of your feet to find the distance between the rows in your garden.

Once you have your plan, you can start planting. Using your finger-length measurements, poke a hole in the soil—that is your planting depth. Drop in the seeds, and cover the hole with dirt. Use your finger-width measurements to space your seeds. Now poke another hole that is the same depth, and

▼ *Water your garden regularly to keep growing plants happy and healthy.*

SO LONG, SLUGS!

Slugs are a garden's number-one pest. A gang of slugs can eat a whole row in one night. They will not only eat your seedlings, but they will also slither underground and find your potatoes. To fight slugs, try a yeast trap. Pour a small amount of sugar water and yeast into a cup. Push the cup into the soil near the plants that the slugs are eating. The slugs will want the mixture more than your plants. When they slide into your yeast trap, they will drown.

▶ *Take care of your garden and you may get juicy, red tomatoes through the summer.*

drop them in. Repeat this until you have a row. Use your foot measurements to space your rows. Water your seeds right away.

Now that your garden is planted, keep watering it and watch it grow. Add compost to the soil to keep it healthy. Lastly, watch out for insect pests. Carrot flies, cabbage flies, slugs, and aphids will eat your veggies before you can. Soon, you will have a beautiful garden full of vegetables that you can eat!

Hands-on Activity: Making a Wormery

Remember how worms are great for your garden? They'll also eat your kitchen scraps and turn them into excellent compost.

What You'll Need:

A glass jar with a lid, sand, soil, earthworms, old leaves, and peelings from vegetables and fruit

Directions:

1. First, clean the glass jar. Then, pour a thin layer of sand into the bottom of the jar. Next, add an inch or two of soil.
2. Then, add another thin layer of sand. After that, add another inch or two of soil. Keep adding these layers until you have filled the jar about halfway.
3. Then, put your earthworms into the jar with some old leaves and vegetable and fruit peelings on top. Put the lid on and poke holes in the top for air.

Worms hate light, so cover the jar in dark material or paper. Also, keep the soil damp—they do not like dry soil. Watch the worms turn the soil by bringing the leaves and peelings down into the dirt.

IN THE GARDEN

21

Glossary

carbon dioxide (KAR-bun dye-OK-siyd): Carbon dioxide is a colorless gas made by the breathing of animals and by the decaying of animal and vegetable matter. Plants absorb carbon dioxide and release oxygen.

climates (CLY-mits): Climates are the average conditions of weather in regions, as shown by temperature, wind speed, and rain. Climates help gardeners decide what they will plant in their gardens.

decomposed (dee-kum-POHZD): A plant is decomposed when it has rotted, broken down, or decayed. Compost is made of decomposed plants.

fiber (FY-bur): Fiber is a substance found in plants, such as fruits and vegetables. Fiber is the part of a fruit or vegetable your body cannot break down.

greenhouse (GREEN-hous): A greenhouse is a structure enclosed in glass and is used to protect and grow plants. Someone in a colder climate may use a greenhouse to grow a garden.

humus (HYOO-mus): Humus is the brown or black substance in soil, made from partly decayed plant or animal matter. Humus is what is left over when plants are decomposed.

nutrients (NOO-tree-ents): A nutrient is any substance that feeds or nourishes a body. Fruits and vegetables contain lots of nutrients.

organic (or-GAN-ik): Something is organic if it is related to or made from living organisms. Organic food is grown without chemicals or pesticides.

oxygen (OK-si-jun): Oxygen is a colorless and odorless gas you need in order to breathe. Plants release oxygen into the air.

particles (PAR-ti-kulz): Particles are tiny pieces, portions, or amounts of something. There are three types of soil particles.

vitamins (VYE-tuh-minz): Vitamins are substances found in foods that our bodies need to function properly. Fruits and vegetables are good sources of vitamins.

To Learn More

BOOKS

Graimes, Nicola. *Kids' Fun and Healthy Cookbook*. New York: DK Publishing, 2007.

Vogel, Julia. *Save the Planet: Local Farms and Sustainable Foods*. Ann Arbor: Cherry Lake Publishing, 2010.

WEB SITES

Visit our Web site for links about gardens: **childsworld.com/links**

Note to Parents, Teachers, and Librarians: We routinely verify our Web links to make sure they are safe and active sites. So encourage your readers to check them out!

Index